Relax
Color
Enjoy

Dedicated to those that Love unconditionally,
be who you are, Love who you are,
Love those around you.

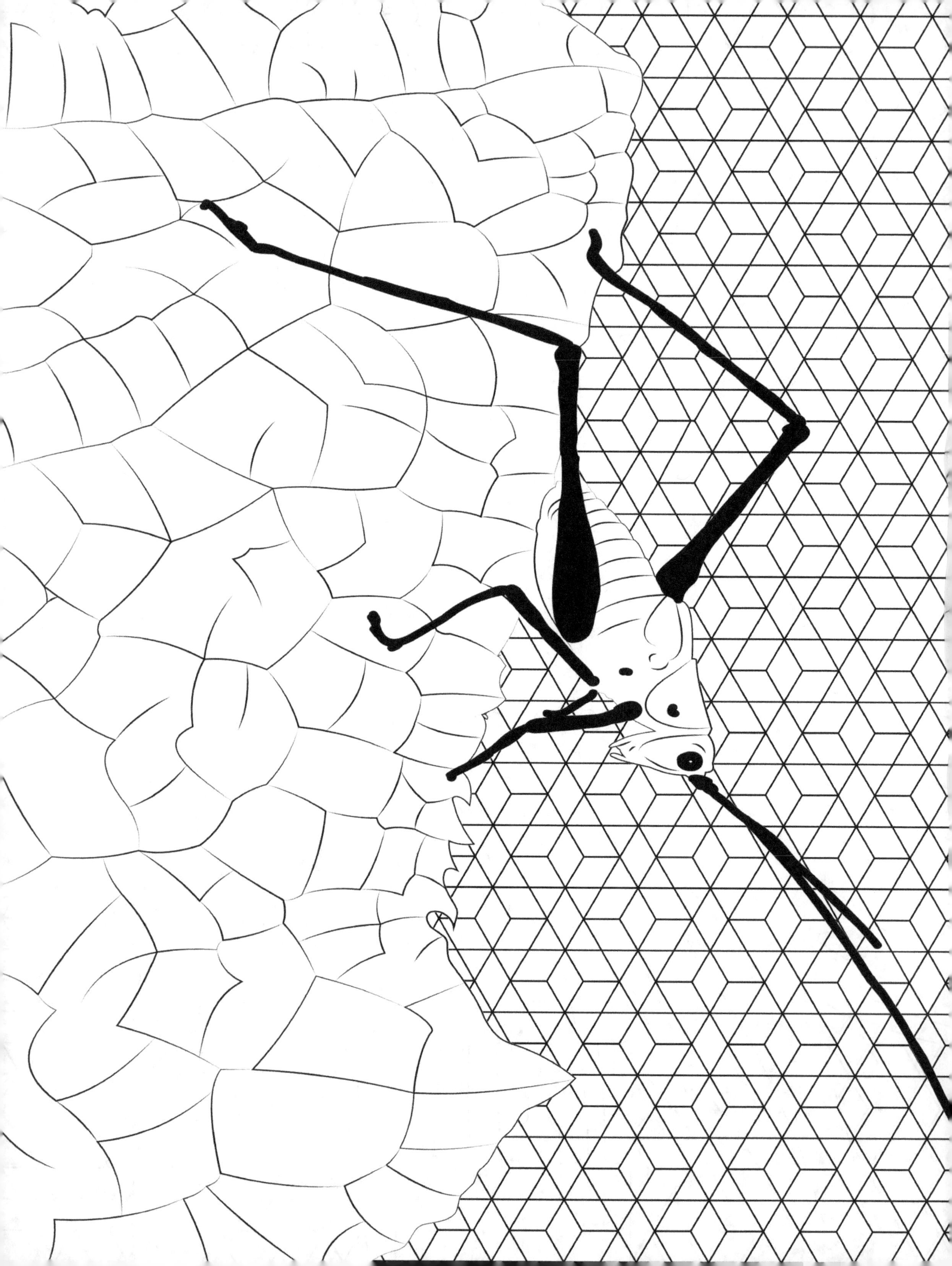

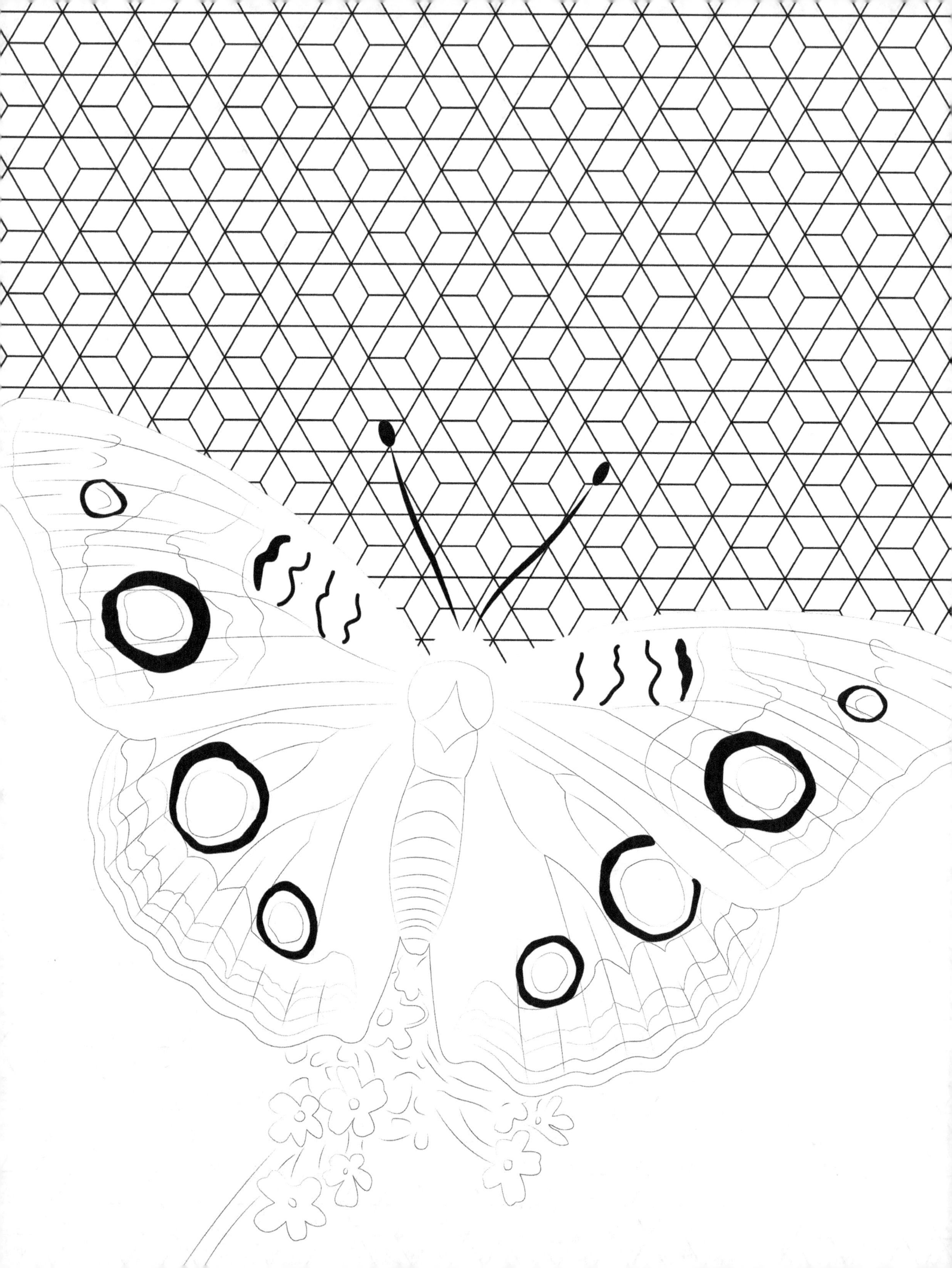

A Little Bit of Nature and Color from Springfield Missouri
A Photo Book By W S Haberthur,
Whimsical Photo Plus Design
Purchase On Amazon

www.ingramcontent.com/pod-product-compliance
Lightning Source LLC
Chambersburg PA
CBHW080049260726
48658CB00007B/2823